A Violet
A Jennifer

poems

Jennifer Badot

LILY POETRY REVIEW BOOKS

Contents

for
Michael Macaluso & Philip David Welsh —
poets gone too soon

Ah, could they know
how violets throw strange fire,
red and purple and gold,
how they glow
gold and purple and red
where her feet tread.

—H.D., *Hymen*

FIRST WORD

Even your wound is a mask
over the older, original wound

and under the jewels, jaws.

So speak. Say you

once lived in a house
with woods behind.

You weren't the first
to trod the path
that wound

beside the pond
with your trickle-
bubble heart,

your ancestors behind
you, pain and music
behind you, a woman

humming you
into being,
stain

of your fathers
inside you,

so speak.

EVERY DOOR A FUROR

The blue house speaks and the dawn speaks

In a windy room
grey-winged

photographs
fly

through air.
Light hides

under the floor.
The man's

hand in
the little

girl's
pants

withdraws
and closes

the door.
The room

rains. The rain
pours.

LOVE AND AMEN

Walk across the clovered
grass to the old stump.
Sit.

Give this tempest
to the ringed
wood, to the brindled

bird cascading down
the sky. Now go
to your writing. Light

a candle and pine
incense. Refuge
of sweet smoke, colored

pencils in jars
the love and amen
of the tangible world.

A GIRL GOES FORTH

I spring from a wound
in a gush of babies
after World War II.

I hardly know the Cold
War. Behind the wall
I make mud, a blue

-eyed girl
in a story. Schooled
that my country

is the mightiest in the world,
I am petrified of men
and murder.

~

I slip
into the glory
of pine and birch,

filaments and frogs,
a pond in winter
that magicks into ice.

My eyes
un-blued
become seers.

I listen
for the dead:
They come

in the mist and
they come
in the thunder.

I am a wild knower.
I am a flower.

WORDS FROM A DREAM

She says,
I'll be leaving Soon:

Soon is a place
the dead go to grieve.

Then she says, *No,*
Soon isn't a place —

it's a bridge
between places.

WHO MADE ME

Earth made you
and mother gave you
a name. A name

is a room with a story:
A man will come
to take your hands

and tell enthralling
lies. Best leave
before he arrives.

Go find the bridge
above the gorge
and hurl your name inside.

GIANT STORY

Listen to the midnight blue crayon

rubbing inside the lines of Sleeping

Beauty's dress. Look, the girl is lying

on her stomach, coloring. Breathe

the orange scent of her mother's

skin. Hear the ironing board

unfold and the sighing

of the iron and the soap

opera's hourglass on the black

and white TV saying *These are*

the days of our lives. Look out

the window to the tawny

tangle of woods. Do you

see the giant walking

toward the house in

his rough brown britches?

Do you see how

he reaches in

and wrenches the girl

from the floor?

GRIEF'S PEOPLE

At the spring equinox my grief spun
the sun's light into small people.

I gathered them and set them
to live in the ground

to tend the seeds,
to pick at them

and burst them.
They were grim

in their work,
though their tiny axes

gleamed. Beneath the new
green that year

a factory of tears
saw the flowers born.

GENERATION

My mother shut me
up with face slaps.
My grandmother
vanquished me
with her eyes
hundreds of times
always
in the kitchen
where my vagina
grew a mouth
and said
this is a farce
instead of *this is good*.
As I failed
hard to please them
I waited for them to go
so that I could
finally speak —
as if the dead
wouldn't hear me,
as if the dead's vaginas
wouldn't grow ears
and listen inside me,
grow tongues
and seethe
and whisper
inside me.

THE SLUT SPEAKS AT THIRTEEN

I'm easy
I've fallen

through the cracks
of god

onto the fields
of shame, singing:

There's a beer can
where a lily pad should be
in a round suburban pond.

~

What I've eaten
I've killed

with my own two hands.
My hands are your hands,

you virgins on the edge
of where no one should go

looking to see what
I'll do next, and who.

~

Night, day, when this sordid
sort of thing happens, you eye

me, inject this dirt
into your blood.

How it excites you —
the way I come

out of the woods
and send boys home to mothers

with the flick of a branch
I've broken from the tree.

~

In the morning, safe
in the safe rustle

of your father's paper
near the bacon-splattered

stove you know your
mother will clean,

you forget me, you think
my body is not your body;

you've been spared, you're clean
and it is my skin into which

bugs burrow and mix
with sperm and unmeant kisses.

~

Your mouths, innocent
won't speak to me

yet you watch me like a movie
you were told not to see,

watch me in the dark
parking lot slip

down into a Chrysler, rock
like a horse with a quarter slot.

~

You watch me disappear
down a path you never knew

was there, wonder where,
in what murky damp place

I linger. You don't know what I know
about the pond and every turtle,

twirling bug and snake in it. I've kissed
the dark tree you can't see

from the road. I've seen you standing
outside the church, baptized

in perfumes and douches, stinking
pretty to heaven, thinking on your knees

that I'm not you, not even loving
me secretly, every scale and tentacle

of me makes you seethe.
I am glorious.

YOU COME AND GO

You come and go, men.
And I hunger or I heed

how to keep you: wait
and entertain, dress

and become. Then the tasks:
hush, hurry, heal.

HOME DECORATING

I seek salvation in the home
decorating magazines my mother
collects. These perfect rooms
with no one in them. I want
their neutrals, their spacious
arrays and brass sconces
splashing way-showing light
on chartreuse walls. I want to perch
on a linen cushion and pen
a sentence to my teachers:
I'm not the dirty mouth you think
me to be. I want my name
to be Mary. Want the teddy bear
to close my vigilant eyes
into the ballerina
jewelry box. I want
the wardrobe mirror
to love me all night long.

.

FIELD

Coming into my mind
for three days now
that field in snow
my wool mittens
wet with snow clumps
Sun arching his back
in asanas
lighting up the land
Pine brushing
her long scented hair
healing me
making of me
a loved child
standing in a field

FLOORPLAN

I was born in a one-story
house with a moss-covered walk.
Two dogs flanked the kitchen.
Snakes and snails swirled in the garden.
Now I'm grown.
The floorplan here is simple:
Entry with octagon-shaped windows
for watching rain, then down
the long hallway, a tomb.
Past it a door
for anyone that leaves.

COOK

I quarter the apples first,
arrange them in a yellow
enamel pot and praise
the solid form
of butter as it melts
around onions (I slice them quick,
ease them off the board into an iron
pan so hot what else matters?)
I waste nothing: skins of fish
I tack to trees in the yard.
Rinds I let dry in heaps
on the hall table. The day
I came to cooking, I'd led
an inconsequential life.
Then the ceremony of
crackling deranged me.

AUDIBLE

A voice beneath vines — a bell
maybe, or music left behind. A sound
like mourning or the melt
of what's frozen, the girl in me
and the woman who lives.
In this place (I *am* a place)
of ground: excavated, new,
broken and waiting
to be broken —
I hear it.

⁓

I hear it under subway tracks
when I cross the river
to go to work; hear it under
fill and silt; under five-thousand-
year-old fish weirs and ancient
spring herring runs; under clay,
scab crust, mantle and the liquid
outer core; hear it all the way
to the inner core which is said
to be made of strange fire.

MOUTH GUARD

With the catalpa tree bright yellow
and the cherry tree umbilical red

With a small candle on my desk
eyeing me,

I detect a loosening
in my mouth — not a tooth
but a thin guard I always knew

was there: I work at it
with my tongue, push it
out, examine the slippery see-through

thing imprinted with dark chewing
and the skeletons of words.

At the back of my throat now
I feel a slithering.

Who goes there?

What could be
so alive?

IF I AM A WOMAN OF THIS EARTH

I'm a basket
and you're holding me.

You're weaving me
a new handle.

You gather and part,
gather and part.

You must be
from home.

How else
can you smooth me?

How do you braid
and reach this far

into what must be
me if I am

a woman of this
earth?

BIVOUAC

What's most blinding
now is my garden — how it expands
in neglect — and what's odd
and renewing is that I'd prayed

for something like this, an end
to epitome and order. I'd lost
the slowness — so much so
that I started to believe

in asking. *Can you propel*
me through the air
into a new and ravenous
quiet? Can you loosen and spill me?

Whatever I build now
will be makeshift, a place
so susceptible to freedom
I won't even sleep there.

THE POET LOCATES HERSELF

[in the yard]

There are vicious plants
with pitfall traps.

There are plants that rip
down the gutter.

What about those knotweed
soldiers commandeering the lawn

or the mock
orange so duplicitous?

Me, I'm a violet,
a soft violet
jaw with a bone.

[in the museum]

Here's the barge known
as the subway that carried me
to and from my office job.

Here's the old Hermes
Rocket typewriter
with broken **S**.

This is the onion skin paper
wrapped around the platen

In the cracked blue

vial, all my words.

[in dream fragments and a question]

twenty-five or thirty years left of
sweet life

~

the enchantment
of the temple is not in
the temple

~

how is your notebook
like a griffin?

[*alarm*]

What I thought were scraps
and detritus

assemble into breaths
become a body.

How wrong I've been —
how grasping: failing

again and again, falling
down, a poet with no hands.

[*a game of alphabet*]

Allocution from a proper Bitch: make this
my Cameo appearance. Defensible,
I am *Enfant terrible,* a Fighter, a Grass

snake, a wannabe Hafez, too.
I Interrupt along the Jawbone. Loud
as a Katydid with my Lecture, one
Mot juste after another poured into
the Notorious Now. I am Open. I live in the Palace
of the Quartz Requiem and I can tell you
it's a Steep Terror, but I am Undying,
not Vanishing. I am a Walkie-talkie
of the deity, a Xyster in the surgery
of the dead. Yea, for I have promised
my hand to the Zygote of my Art.

[*the right pen*]

With my pen dipped in YES
I listen to the singing

It sings *crush   crush   crush*

       It sings *Ma   Ma   Ma*

   It sings   *Ssssssssssssssssssssssssss*

     It sings *Haaaaaaaaaaaaaaaaaaa!*

[*dawn*]

every poem
a door
a door
opened
not by speaking
by listening
to a hundred
thousand songs
singing the one
that shines

SPELL FOR A PERFECTIONIST

Into your taxidermy shop
where you skin, hollow
arrange, sew (blood-let
innards hung, silver fir
needle-stung) I pour
gold water, strum
of bees, Saint Joan's
fevered hair. Give you
sensing, mewling yellow eyes
all shot through with gnosis,
stars. Give you nerve, beat,
slime, webbed feet. I shawl
your sharp shoulders, spit
your flesh, spill you
wild honey, I spell
you wrong.

CHERRY STREET

Every day it was another deity.
I saw Erzulie as I dressed for work.
She followed me down Cherry St.
and had me exchange my love-grief
for subway tokens and Venus
lay around on Sundays eating
whatever Sekhmet cooked (spicy
blackened meat over oil-glistened greens,
pomegranate glazes, orange cremes).
Year of mornings, the kitchen floor
sticky with honey, Brigid stirred
my coffee into light and I tried
to write but could only quiver
and plunge yolk-coated plates
into warm suds, hang my rage
on the back of the door
draw a bath.

MUSE

You know me so
come fast
from your blue loom
of sky and hitch
on the hem of my skirt
sewn in Jiangsu. Let's blow
these fluorescent places and go *au*
naturale or walk about
as beams of light and filter
the air of gloom. How
is the earth so wet? And look
at green vrooming beside the freeway
glinting love and Autumn
just over there saddling up
the maple mare with gold
and crimson blankets.

RED MARE

This morning I wake with viscera
on my mind. The viscera is mine,
underneath the skin-of-me wet
and warm like a stew. Muscle
and bone too, these hefts
in my chest, my chest
torn open. In a girlhood
closet I secreted an apple
to make a doll. I watched it
shrivel and gnarl into a face
then gave the doll a story.
I told it against the scenery
of my body at first lying
and then telling myself
not to lie. I scared myself:
She rode *la mer rouge* of my blood.
She rode a red mare through all
the parts of my heart — *Atrium, Bundle
of His, Vena Cava.* In the paddock
of my mouth she lassoed
my breath. She made me
scream. She bid me *Ride.*

AT CALDERWOOD NECK

Blue pythons rolling ever
on the incoming. The girl
with windmill eyes
is sad she's going to die
and the wind is already
blowing. Last night
in the woods rain
flooded the land. Grass
heads crown the muddy
pools; they are the drowned
ones laden with grace. The sea
is flesh and flesh
upon flesh. White hats
on blue skulls. Fish blood
and rune spells. Green jade
snake on the path first
an O then an S then away.
Death is the light on the outgoing.

AUGUST DREAM

Two women are swimming
at night. One of them
is me. The other is older
and braver: she dives
down and I know
I'm to follow. The water
is salty, pulmonary. I'm afraid
of depth so I stay on the surface
then force myself down,
first my head, then the rest
of me slipping in, a reverse
birth. My comfort is in
the nearness of the old one
at ease in this element
and her own flesh.

SKETCH OF THE RIVER

Just one scant length of it
from a rock to an arching pine
a few dozen girl-steps at most
nowhere really
merely a run
of rooted brown
water greeted
by columbine
but there was my breath
mingling with Earth's!

MOTHERBOARD

Those were the years of away
between rain and rain

and the blue spear
of land and the cry of waters,

when green smoke
wended wet

and seeds were riven
and my hands

pulled over and under
a gleaming contraption.

With grit and shine
I harvested, stitched

and laid by packages.
I built a store.

And as each need
lit up my board

I delivered,
I delivered.

YOU WHO WERE GIVEN

You who were given a life, what did you make of it?

I dug holes
with a stick, joined a water bug
council, twirled on the black water
was dispersed, prayed
for help to come, then gave
myself over to it.

I cut the ends off
green beans, held
the door open. I stirred
the soup, edited
mended, clapped, reflected —

bridled, broke.

You who were given
What did you make?

RETURNING TO THE GIRL

Returning
to my girl body. Returning to my poem
body, my green body. My woman body
and my girl body side by side walking,
side by side climbing into my girl bed.
Climbing into my bed, into my poem bed.
My woman bed and my girl bed side by side
beneath the window and the poem bed
near the door, the green blanket,
the fire burning, my poem body
turning on top of the bed, my girl
body opening the door.

BIRTHDAY

Light trusses
my body to space.

Hawk's taut eye
is grave toward sky.

Ice forms
a hard caul.

~

With my mother
in her anesthetic sleep
I am born at sunrise
near the winter
solstice with a caul.

(Is that why
I'll want
to sleep
alone, a
rover,
a stranger?)

~

A violet
a jennifer
what does
a girl
traveling
down
the darkness
seek?

FIELD NOTE

Honey-colored doe leaps into pines

No rain for weeks
and the pond is low

A hermit thrush way up
enchants   enchants

Sun hot and long
golden grass
on the path
heralds you

Here I've made
these cakes
for you
I'll leave them floating
on the water

LAMMAS EVE

twenty-five or thirty years
left of sweet life

~

I am hummed
and beholden

I am spilled
from your cornucopia

with no authority
whatsoever

into bread
knead me

couple me
with wine

take me
into your

sun spun
arms

sweet
green
tree
freedom

absolute
rose in
the center

MAY DAY

I'm eleven I just got loved
I wish I knew what an enemy does
He said there's no such thing
as an enemy. His button said
Make Love Not War. He told
jokes. He fixed my bike. He played
our piano. He could sing.
I told him my mother was working.
I told him my father doesn't live
with us. He told me I'm beautiful.
He said I'll love you. I said I write
poems. He said let's see. I said the light
is broken. He said we won't need
the light. My sister didn't like him. He's older
than her. My sister screamed. He locked
the door. I said do you like fries McDonald's
is opening up. He laughed. He put his hand
down my pants. He laughed again. Everytime
he laughed it hurt. He said I love you.
I never saw him before. My sister
banged on the door. I told him
not to love me anymore
but he just wouldn't stop.

NOTES ON HYMEN

Vestigial rose bouquet

Magma of trauma

Do you remember how they entered
first the door then
how they opened me and closed me
opened me
closed me
and closed me?

~

Maybe you're in California
or maybe on the death star.
I see you near a fire
dreaming
of what I'll say
when I'm bridle-less
and can blow words
through my pearly moon
conch shell flute. Come
to me, my invisible companion, I'm
so lonely. Let's go
naked or wear the same rag
for days and not brush
our teeth. Our apple-ferment gums
will gleam. Tonight, though it's
morning

now, we'll run down
Cherry St. toward rage.
We'll grind the air,
throw your green blanket
over us, leave
our tongues exposed.

NOTES

"You Who Were Given"
This poem is indebted to the question posed in Forrest Gander's poem, "What It Sounds Like" — You who were given a life, what did you make of it?

"Notes on Hymen"
A most grateful acknowledgement to Dawn Lundy Martin whose prompt and encouragement fostered the writing of this poem.

ACKNOWLEDGEMENTS

Thank you to the following publications where several of these poems originally appeared: Boston Phoenix Literary Supplement: "Bivouac"; The Boston Globe: "Cook"; Lily Poetry Review: "Floorplan" and "Grief's People."

My deepest gratitude to the following people who have encouraged and celebrated my poetic eruptions over the years: Elizabeth Badot Besser, Kathryn Deputat, Phebe Eckfeldt, Steve Goldenberg & Mimi Simmons, Ali Harris, Victoria Hood, Sarah Anne Johnson, LK, Eugenie Kuffler, Rabbi Em Mueller, Doug Selwyn & Jan Maher, and Kathy & Howard Shapiro.

Gratitude to my early teachers Martha Collins and Lloyd Schwartz whose support and warmth continues to nourish me. Gratitude also to Spencer Reece with whom I kept a sacred appointment, and Laura Smith-Riva who has stood by me in the breach. Thank you to Gloria Mindock, Editor of Červená Barva Press, for her support and for hosting the Poets Round Table where many of these poems were shared aloud for the first time. Thanks to everyone at The Home School and to Tom Daley and the poets at his inimitable table — Kelly DuMar, Jenny Grassl, Cathy Morrocco, Gale Batchelder, Paul Nemser, Judson K. Evans, Robin Linn and Catherine Broderick — for their astute reading and camaraderie when I was emerging after a long silence. Thank you to Robert Carr, whose generous and thoughtful attention to this work came at a crucial moment.

I am beyond grateful to Eileen Cleary, Poetry Angel Extraordinaire, who saw this book before I did, and to everyone at Lily Poetry Review Books, without whom this book would not be in your hands right now.

Special thanks to J. Johnson, whose music fills our home and my heart. Tenderness and love to my parents, stepparents, and my entire family, especially my sons Julian and Samuel who pour all the meaning into "my pride and joy."

Finally, thank you, dear reader. I hope you found one or two morsels here to sustain you.

About the author

Jennifer Badot is the author of the chapbook *Poem for the Fire and other Kindling.* Her poems and prose have appeared in *Studia Mystica,* the *Boston Globe,* the Boston Phoenix Literary Supplement, Lily Poetry Review and elsewhere. She lives in Massachusetts with her human, animal and plant family.

CPSIA information can be obtained
at www.ICGtesting.com
Printed in the USA
LVHW052333230322
714086LV00016B/3298